STEP ELEVEN

Centering Ourselves

First published August, 1983

Printed in the United States of America.

The following is an adaptation of one of the Twelve Steps in the program of Overeaters Anonymous. It is one person's interpretation and does not speak for the O.A. organization.

The heart of the program

Step Eleven spells out what we have been trying to do all along, perhaps even before we found the Overeaters Anonymous program. The presence of a Higher Power is a reality deep within each one of us, attracting our consciousness like a magnetic field. In the Eleventh Step, we reaffirm our desire and decision to know and do the will of this Higher Power. Through prayer and meditation, we want to improve our conscious contact with the God of our understanding.

How we take this Step is a choice which we make according to individual preference. There are many ways to pray and meditate, and each of us is free to have a personal understanding of a Higher Power. The program is big and broad enough to accommodate all of us, since the only requirement of O.A. membership is the desire to stop overeating.

What makes the Twelve Step programs uniquely effective is that they offer a guide to spiritual growth. When we find that we cannot stop overeating compulsively without coming to know and rely on a power greater than ourselves, we see how Step Eleven is central to our plan of recovery. Though practice of the Step may be sporadic at first, we will keep returning to it because it works. Many of us are convinced that our periods of prayer and meditation have become the best time of the day, and that regular use of the Eleventh Step is the heart of our recovery program. In these quiet moments, we recharge our batteries by getting in touch with the source of our strength, and we find direction for our lives one day at a time. Prayer and meditation keep us alive and growing.

Centering

If prayer and meditation are new to you, consider that you are embarking on an inner voyage of exploration and discovery. If "the only scoffers at prayer are those who never tried it enough,"* then making a commitment to practice Step Eleven on a daily basis will be a way of demonstrating its effectiveness in your life. When we are willing to try to improve our conscious contact with a Higher Power, we are open to whatever insight comes our way, and the longer we work the O.A. program, the more we become convinced that each day we are given exactly what we need.

Beginning the morning with a few quiet minutes gets us together and links us up with a source of strength and peace beyond ourselves. One way to start is with the Serenity Prayer: "God, grant me the serenity to accept the things I cannot change, the courage to change the things I can, and the wisdom to know the difference."

*Twelve Steps and Twelve Traditions, published by A.A. World Services, New York, NY, p. 97. Available through Hazelden Educational Materials.

Many of us use one or more of the daily meditation books which have been published for members of Twelve Step programs. After reading the thought for the day, which may include a short prayer, some of us like to let our minds be quiet and take time to listen for an inner voice.

It has been suggested that prayer is asking a question and meditation is listening for the answer. At the beginning, we may spend most of our time telling our Higher Power what is going on and where we are. Gradually, we learn to center ourselves and be receptive to the thoughts and feelings that rise gently from down deep instead of chasing those that are spinning around the top of our head. This has been described as thinking God's thoughts after Him.

With practice, prayer and meditation become tools for an ongoing relationship that recreates us each time we make contact. We know that we are in touch with the spiritual base of our lives, and we don't have to do, say, or think anything. We can just **be.**

As compulsive overeaters, many of us pray first of all for abstinence: **If it is your will, God, give me abstinence just for today. I cannot do it alone.** We can come back to this prayer as often as necessary. It reminds us that we have turned over our will and our lives, along with our abstinence. Each time we remember, we are touching base and centering ourselves in a Higher Power.

Meditation for serenity

What, for some of us, used to be periods of anxiety and terror can become times of creative meditation and spiritual growth. Although abstinence from compulsive overeating is our goal, this does not automatically guarantee tranquility. It often happens that the fears we have tried to suppress with excess food will push to the surface of our awareness when we stop using food as a tranquilizer. If we are not going to eat over this fear, what are we going to do? What do you do when you wake up in the middle of the night gripped by a nameless anxiety or convinced of some impending disaster?

If we believe that a Higher Power has put us where we are for a reason and that we are in exactly the place we should be, then we can partially detach ourselves from the emotional storm that is raging inside, and we can wait quietly for it to pass. In the process we will undoubtedly learn something we did not know before, or something we knew but would not face. The fears we try to avoid and deny are the ones which develop into panic. Let your fear surface. Give it a name. Be willing to feel it. Then ask yourself if the God of your understanding wants you to be afraid.

Since your Higher Power is in charge of your life, you are not alone with whatever it is you face. Moment by moment, you will be given the strength you need. We lose jobs and loved ones. We live with frustration and illness. Chaos may appear to swirl around us, but if our inner perception is grounded in God's reality, here and now, we will not be swept away by fear and panic or try to escape through overeating.

With daily practice, the quiet time of meditation extends order to the busy hours and begins to erase irrational fears. As we go deeper into the stillness within, we find ourselves in a place where there is increasing love and decreasing fear. If we go **through** our fear, not trying to cover it up or escape, we will come out on the other side realizing that the fear was not a solid wall after all.

The key which unlocks the treasure of Step Eleven is regular use. We set aside a definite period of time every day when we will be available to our Higher Power, and we follow whatever individual plan we have for prayer and meditation, whether or not we feel like it. Call it spiritual exercise, if you wish. Serenity is a spiritual muscle which is developed with training and concentration. It does not fall into our lap out of the blue. If we want the inner peace and serenity which come from conscious contact with the God of our understanding, we have to be willing to take the time to cultivate the relationship. Remembering the "condition of complete simplicity costing not less than everything," we may have to postpone or eliminate some of our other activities if they get in the way.

First things first

Setting priorities is essential if we are to work the steps of the program and maintain abstinence from compulsive overeating. Since millions of stimuli compete every day for our attention and energy, there is no way we can or should act on more than a tiny fraction of the ideas, impulses, requests, desires, and demands which present themselves. If we go off in all directions, the resulting fatigue and chaos not only destroy serenity but also threaten abstinence.

The minutes we spend quietly getting in touch with ourselves and our Higher Power will multiply our effectiveness in everything we do throughout the day. When we are focused and integrated, we get to the heart of whatever needs to be done without wasting unnecessary time and effort. How often did you spin your wheels getting nowhere when you were overeating? The disorder and frustration of those days can be put behind you now that you have a program for living and a way to sort out what is important.

If you wake up in the morning and don't know where to start or how you can possibly do all the things you think ought to be done, ask for help. Ask your Higher Power to direct your thoughts and your actions, setting your priorities for the next twenty-four hours. Ask again and again during the day, whenever you feel confused. Remember that the answer is not likely to be found in the refrigerator.

As we go through the steps to recovery, we examine our lives and find that in many cases what used to be important and time-consuming is no longer of much value. Trying to impress others, grasping all we can get, winning arguments and being right, hanging on to the past, trying to rearrange the world to suit us — this compulsive behavior is tiring and self-defeating. When we are in contact with a reality beyond our own ego, we can spontaneously live each moment according to inner direction and "go with the flow" instead of trying to swim upstream. Our priorities are sorted out according to what seems right in relation to a Higher Power.

Letting God determine what is important may appear to be a somewhat shaky and frightening procedure at first. What if it doesn't work? On the other hand, how well did we do when we were following the dictates of self-will? Being open and willing to try what has worked for other people in the program has brought us this far and will take us through Step Eleven. We may not be able to explain how prayer and meditation work, but when we experience firsthand the positive difference they make in our lives, we will have a growing faith in their effectiveness.

Learning what we need to do in order to maintain abstinence and stay on the track emotionally and spiritually is an experience of trial and error and self-discovery. We are not likely to be struck by thunderbolts of revelation or see burning bushes during our periods of meditation. What we do encounter is a slowly growing sense of assurance and relatedness, faith that we are being cared for and directed. Returning to this inner place several times each day becomes a number one priority, the starting point from which everything else falls into place.

To know God's will

When we get tangled up in conflicting shoulds, oughts, and wants, it helps to remember that Step Eleven suggests we pray "only for knowledge of God's will for us and the power to carry that out."* This simple recommendation cuts a straight path through a maze of anxiety and indecision. It is a direct route to serenity.

If we decide ahead of time what we want for ourselves, or someone else, or the state of the union, and if we pray for that to happen, we will probably be disappointed and disillusioned if events turn out otherwise. If we had all the answers, we would not need a Higher Power. The fact of the matter is, we often do not know what is best for ourselves, other people, or the world in general, and even if we did, we do not have the ability to manipulate external events. Trying to run even our own small corner of the world is a wearisome and defeating experience.

How much more rewarding it is to pray that God's will be done, since that puts us on the side of reality! Thinking in terms of God's will rather than self-will means that we can relax our efforts to figure everything out. If we pray sincerely to know what our Higher Power wants us to do in a given situation, we can assume that the answer will come without a lot of worry and indecision. It may not come today, but

---

*Ibid, p. 102.

when we need to act, we can trust that we will be guided. In the meantime, a good rule of thumb is: when in doubt, don't. When action is necessary, we do the best we can according to the insight we possess at the time, and if we make a mistake we can try again.

How do we know God's will for our lives? How can we be sure that we are not rationalizing our own desires into the will of a Higher Power? Here is where the support of other people in the program becomes an important part of Step Eleven. We do not have to make far-reaching decisions by ourselves. Someone we trust can be a sounding board when we are not sure which course of action to take. Believing that a Higher Power works through other people also, we can expect to have many of our questions answered through dialogue with those who are our companions in this spiritual journey.

Another test is that of time. If we are headed in the wrong direction, we're going to realize it sooner or later. The longer and more conscientiously we work the steps, the earlier we are able to recognize and correct a faulty course of action.

Experience indicates that we get into trouble when we try to see too far ahead. We do not need to know God's will for us for next week or next year or the rest of our lives. Since this is a one-day-at-a-time program, we are only concerned with knowing and doing the will of a Higher Power now, today. We can pray that our thoughts and actions today will be on target and leave the future in God's hands.

We can also leave in God's hands His will for other people. We are "praying only for knowledge of His will for us." The decision of what is best for someone else is not ours to make, difficult as it may be to let go. Even when we are convinced that we know what someone close to us should or should not do, the program teaches us to detach with love. We respect each individual's right to live his or her own life. Though we may do all we can to help those we care about, the ultimate responsibility rests between them and the God of their understanding.

Power to do it

Most of us have more than a glimmer of an idea of what God's will for us might include. The crunch comes when we think about actually carrying out some of these possibilities. Often, we find ourselves in a position where "the spirit is willing but the flesh is weak."

As an example, we may assume that our Higher Power's will for us is abstinence from compulsive overeating and from emotional and spiritual destruction. In Step Eleven we pray for the power to do our part in maintaining this abstinence. It is not enough to know what is good for us; we need to do the footwork which brings about the desired results. Prayer and meditation can be done by ourselves, but this does not mean that we no longer need the strength of the group to maintain our program of recovery.

Whatever we focus on for the day, we will be sustained in our efforts by the fact that others are working along similar lines. After you have asked for the power to be abstinent, make a phone call to reinforce your intent. Get to a meeting if you feel yourself slipping into an emotional binge. There is strength in the fellowship which carries over into the times when we are alone and unsure.

Often, the courage to take the first faltering step on a

course of action will generate the power to take another step, and another, and another. The miracle of this program is the positive change it effects in our lives. When we are willing to move ahead, however tentatively, growth is possible. We make the first move toward a new job, a new relationship, a new commitment, not knowing exactly what the outcome will be but with the faith that we will have guidance and strength to continue, if it is God's will.

The Eleventh Step points our way toward becoming a channel for the action of a Higher Power. Time spent improving our conscious contact means that we will have something to pass on to the people with whom we interact. Increasingly, we come to believe that the challenges and blessings of each day are ours for a reason. Other people cross our paths because we have something to give them and receive from them. Don't forget, we are no longer trying to run the show. Since we are sincerely seeking to know God's will, we can ask for the insight to give and receive at a deeply meaningful level.

We came into Overeaters Anonymous admitting that we were powerless over food and unable to manage our own lives. We declared physical, emotional, and spiritual bankruptcy. Gradually, we are building a new life based on a power beyond ourselves. Insights come, and along with them comes the strength to act on these insights. Our willingness to act and the actions themselves give rise to new insights. We learn and we become stronger, whether our efforts are directed toward following a food plan or determining what other things we need to do in order to like ourselves and live with those around us. Power to do God's will is available to us. Our job is to ask for it — often — and use it.

Wearing the world as a loose garment

"We have found that the actual good results of prayer are beyond question. They are matters of knowledge and experience. All those who have persisted have found strength not ordinarily their own. They have found wisdom beyond their usual capability. And they have increasingly found a peace of mind which can stand firm in the face of difficult circumstances."*

Difficult circumstances have a way of cropping up persistently. None of us is exempt. What we are offered in this program, especially through Step Eleven, is a way of life which keeps us from being overwhelmed and from turning to excess food as a crutch. Friends die and bills pile up. Accidents, injuries, and conflicts are an inevitable part of being alive. Through prayer and meditation we can find a center of calm beneath the daily turbulence. We will still feel grief, pain, anxiety, and anger, but these emotions will not blind or destroy us. Conscious contact with the God of our understanding gives us a core of serenity which no amount of trouble can shatter.

Our serenity may be temporarily submerged by pressing concerns, but we know it still exists in that quiet place within and that all we have to do is take time to go back there. Storms will come, but they will pass. Experience shows us

---

*Ibid, p. 104.

that the sooner we turn the problems over to a Higher Power, the sooner we get back to serenity. The less we allow ourselves to be caught up in the pursuit of possessions, prestige, material security, and ego satisfaction, the more inner peace we will have. This is wearing the world as a loose garment.

Material satisfactions by themselves are not enough. We need daily spiritual nourishment in order to stay strong and healthy. When we give priority to getting ourselves together spiritually, the rest of the world slides into place — loosely and without pressure. We cope with the problems and logistics of our existence without getting bogged down in secondary considerations and without overeating. If we are praying only for the knowledge of God's will for our lives and the power to carry that out, we will not fall apart if someone we love leaves us or if we lose a job. We will hurt; we will be afraid; but we will not be destroyed.

Improving our conscious contact with a Higher Power makes life an adventure instead of a chore. We get in touch with the source of our own creativity. We see new options. We gain the courage to take risks and exercise these creative options. We will have failures and we will have successes, but whatever the results, we are grounded in a source of strength and power beyond ourselves.